The Urbana Free Library

To renew: call 217-367-4057
or go to "urbanafreelibrary.org"
and select "Renew/Request Items"

Rows of Roses

of

by Rebecca Felix

amicus readers

Ideas for Parents and Teachers

Amicus Readers let children practice reading informational texts at the earliest reading levels. Familiar words and concepts with close photo-text matches support early readers.

Before Reading
- Discuss the cover photo with the child. What does it tell him?
- Ask the child to predict what she will learn in the book.

Read the Book
- "Walk" through the book and look at the photos. Let the child ask questions.
- Read the book to the child, or have the child read independently.

After Reading
- Use the matching quiz at the end of the book to review the text.
- Prompt the child to make connections. Ask: *Can you think of other words that sound the same but have different meanings and spellings?*

Amicus Readers are published by Amicus
P.O. Box 1329, Mankato, MN 56002
www.amicuspublishing.us

Library of Congress Cataloging-in-Publication Data

Felix, Rebecca, 1984-
  Rows of roses / Rebecca Felix.
    pages cm -- (Hear homophones here)
  Audience: K to Grade 3.
  Audience: Age 6
  ISBN 978-1-60753-572-0 (hardcover) --
  ISBN 978-1-60753-656-7 (pdf ebook)
  1. English language--Homonyms--Juvenile literature. I. Title.
  PE1595.F47 2014
  428.1--dc23
                              2013048618

Photo Credits: Shutterstock Images, cover, 1, 3, 4–5, 6, 14, 16 (top left), 16 (middle left), 16 (middle right), 16 (bottom left); iStockphoto, 7, 16 (bottom right); Dennis Donohue/Thinkstock, 8; Vaclav Volrab/Shutterstock Images, 9; Maurizio Bonora/Thinkstock, 10–11, 16 (top right); Marcus Siebert/SuperStock, 12 (left); Bowen Clause Photography/Shutterstock Images, 12–13; Vishnevskiy Vasily/Shutterstock Images, 15

Produced for Amicus by The Peterson Publishing Company and Red Line Editorial.

Editor Jenna Gleisner
Designer Jake Nordby
Printed in the United States of America
Mankato, MN
1-2014
PA10001
10 9 8 7 6 5 4 3 2 1

Homophones are words that sound the same. But they have different meanings and spellings. We can find homophones when we look outside.

3

rose
rows

A **rose** is a flower. A **rose** grows on a bush. We plant **rows** of **rose** bushes in the garden.

beech
beach

A **beach** is a sandy edge next to water. A **beech** is a tall tree. This **beech** tree grows near a **beach**.

peak
peek

The top of a mountain is the **peak**. To look at something in secret is to **peek**. This snow leopard will **peek** for food from the mountain **peak**.

9

hare
hair

A **hare** looks like a rabbit. A **hare** has **hair** called fur.

bare
bear

Bare means not covered. A **bear** rubs its back on a tree. The tree looks **bare** without bark.

paws
pause

Bears grow big **paws** with claws. A **pause** is a stop before starting again. Small animals **pause** and hide from big bear **paws**!

Match each homophone to its picture!

beach

beech

hair

hare

rose

rows